# tired of being tired

## study guide

# tired of being tired

## study guide

RECEIVE GOD'S REALISTIC REST
FOR YOUR SOUL-DEEP EXHAUSTION

Jess Connolly

BakerBooks
*a division of Baker Publishing Group*
Grand Rapids, Michigan

Published by Baker Books
a division of Baker Publishing Group
Grand Rapids, Michigan
BakerBooks.com

Printed in the United States of America



Library of Congress Cataloging-in-Publication Data
Names: Connolly, Jess, author.
Title: Tired of being tired study guide : receive God's realistic rest for our soul-deep exhaustion / Jess Connolly.
Description: Grand Rapids, Michigan : Baker Books, a division of Baker Publishing Group, [2024]
Identifiers: LCCN 2023036726 | ISBN 9781540902511 (paperback) | ISBN 9781493444892 (ebook)
Subjects: LCSH: Christian women—Religious life. | Fatigue. | Women—Health and hygiene.
Classification: LCC BV4527 .C643956 2024 | DDC 248.8/43—dc23/eng/20231120
LC record available at https://lccn.loc.gov/2023036726



Study guide written by Abby Perry with additional material by Jess Connolly.

The author is represented by Illuminate Literary Agency, www.IlluminateLiterary.com.

Baker Publishing Group publications use paper produced from sustainable forestry practices and postconsumer waste whenever possible.

24 25 26 27 28 29 30 7 6 5 4 3 2 1

# contents

# how to use this guide

This guide was created to accompany the book *Tired of Being Tired: Receive God's Realistic Rest for Your Soul-Deep Exhaustion*. While you can complete the guide without reading the book, I recommend enhancing your experience by pairing them together.

Each session of the guide correlates with a few chapters of *Tired of Being Tired*. If you're reading as an individual, take your time. Read, reflect, and respond in a way that embodies the very rest you hope to find in these pages.

If you are reading in a group, have an honest conversation with one another about the pace that will work best for each of you. If a six-week structure is too short a time frame for everyone to stay on top of reading and reflecting, consider a twelve- or even eighteen-week structure. The heart of the book and study guide is to help one another find rest, not to increase burdens or to-do lists. Choose a structure that infuses grace and peace into the group before you even begin to read or meet.

## Session Structure

This guide contains six sessions, each with the following sections:

- A Note from Jess
- Savor the Scripture
- Read and Reflect
- Guided Journaling
- Symptom Checker
- Low Power Mode Plan
- Set the Script
- Community Questions
- Prayer

The Community Questions sections assume that you're completing the study in a group setting, such as a Bible study, community group, or book club. If you're reading and studying independently, feel free to answer those questions on your own!

## For Group Leaders

If you are facilitating a group of women working through this study guide, first of all, thank you! While I celebrate those who choose to read individually, I have a great love for the conversations and healing I know can take place when women gather to read, study, pray, and talk with one another.

I encourage you to begin each group session by reading the note from me aloud or asking another group member to do so. Then, read the Savor the Scripture passage aloud and facilitate a moment of silent reflection, which you can conclude by praying aloud for your time together. From there, move into the Community Questions.

Please be sure to emphasize the importance of kindness and confidentiality within the group. Encourage all participants to listen carefully, share honestly, and be trustworthy stewards of one another's stories. Personally, I'd love to suggest a "no unsolicited advice" rule. If someone asks for life wisdom and insight, share generously; otherwise, refraining from advice-giving makes space for compassion and care in a powerful way.

# session *one*

First: Read *Tired of Being Tired* chapters 1–3.

## A Note from Jess

Dear friend,

Let's start honestly, shall we? We're tired. Maybe so tired that we're wondering why we thought starting something new (this study) was a good idea.

Our hair isn't clean. Or it is but our floors aren't. Or they are but our inbox isn't. Or all of that looks great at the same time (tell me your secret!), but that one intangible item on our to-do list—the one that reads something like "help daughter with her anxiety" or "maintain a good relationship with my in-laws" or "find work that creates joy and income at the same time"—has us feeling downright weary no matter how polished our outward appearance.

I'm relatively confident that something in the above paragraph resonates with you for a pretty simple reason: You chose to work through a study guide called *Tired of Being Tired*. Whether you did so out of personal interest, because a friend suggested it, or thanks to your church's choice of curriculum, the truth is that you have a book about tiredness in your hands. I've yet to meet a woman who can't, in some way, relate to the idea of utter exhaustion. Whether you're in a season of acute physical weariness or you're enduring spiritual fatigue that's hard to name, this initial session is going to help you take stock of your energy (or lack of it).

If you take anything from this first session, take this sentence from chapter 1 of *Tired of Being Tired*:

> Jesus didn't purchase our freedom for a life of fatigue, so there has got to be more than an endless cycle of exhaustion.

I believe that truth with my whole heart because I've seen it in Scripture, in my own life, and in the stories of countless women. I believe it for you too.

Jess

## Savor the Scripture

Whether individually or in a group setting, read this passage aloud, then set a one-minute timer for meditating on it silently.

> Are you tired? Worn out? Burned out on religion? Come to me. Get away with me and you'll recover your life. I'll show you how to take a real rest. Walk with me and work with me—watch how I do it. Learn the unforced rhythms of grace. I won't lay anything heavy or ill-fitting on you. Keep company with me and you'll learn to live freely and lightly. (Matt. 11:28–30 MSG)

Which word or phrase from the passage is sticking with you after the meditation moment? Jot it down as a guiding theme for the rest of the session.

## Read and Reflect

Then God said, "Let us make mankind in our image, in our likeness, so that they may rule over the fish in the sea and the birds in the sky, over the livestock and all the wild animals, and over all the creatures that move along the ground."

> So God created mankind in his own image,
> in the image of God he created them;
> male and female he created them.

God blessed them and said to them, "Be fruitful and increase in number; fill the earth and subdue it. Rule over the fish in the sea and the birds in the sky and over every living creature that moves on the ground."

Then God said, "I give you every seed-bearing plant on the face of the whole earth and every tree that has fruit with seed in it. They will be yours for food. And to all the beasts of the earth and all the birds in the sky and all the creatures that move along the ground—everything that has the breath of life in it—I give every green plant for food." And it was so.

God saw all that he had made, and it was very good. And there was evening, and there was morning—the sixth day.

Thus the heavens and the earth were completed in all their vast array.

By the seventh day God had finished the work he had been doing; so on the seventh day he rested from all his work. Then God

> blessed the seventh day and made it holy, because on it he rested from all the work of creating that he had done. (Gen. 1:26–2:3)

What do you observe about God in this passage?

What do you observe about us, His children, in this passage?

If humanity is made in God's image, what does that mean for our patterns of work and rest?

## Guided Journaling

Read (or reread) this section from chapter 2, considering it as you journal your thoughts in response to the questions below.

> I don't know what will happen in your life after you embrace realistic, biblical, lasting rhythms of rest. But here's what could happen:
>
> Things could get better.
>
> You could feel more connected to God as your Father, Friend, and daily Companion.
>
> You could feel at home in your body, at peace with your own pace.
>
> You might understand the gospel better, the good gift you've been given to set you free.
>
> You might have a better understanding of your purpose and place in the kingdom.
>
> You could see what your body feels like when you're not always exhausted.
>
> You might feel freer when you stop trying to be everything to everyone.
>
> There's a chance you could experience healing from over-responsibility and imposter syndrome.
>
> I believe you might get a handle on your mental health if you begin to rest.
>
> Your mind might feel easier to quiet and your thoughts more manageable to process.
>
> You could experience the peace that passes understanding, even amid chaos.
>
> If you began to rest consistently and realistically, you could feel more whole emotionally.
>
> You could feel your feelings and live less distracted and compartmentalized.
>
> You could feel capable of encountering great and hard days with your emotions as a help, not a hindrance.

Your spiritual, physical, mental, and emotional well-being could improve if you embrace rest—but they will absolutely all get worse if you don't.

But I've staked my life on the truth of God's Word, and I've found it to be true. And He's got a boatload of promises that are ours for the taking if we will receive the rest He's offering. More than that, I've seen the empirical evidence in my life and others' that if we keep running forward exhausted—it will get worse.

How do you feel about your current patterns of work and rest?

If you could change anything about the way you experience energy or tiredness right now, what would it be?

Where do you feel stuck in your relationship with energy or exhaustion?

## Symptom Checker

In the upcoming sessions, we'll pay close attention to four specific areas of exhaustion: spiritual, physical, mental, and emotional.

For now, simply jot down your initial reaction to each category, stream-of-consciousness style. Try to lift your pen from the page only when you're moving from one type of exhaustion to the next. In other words, share your unfiltered thoughts about how each type of exhaustion shows up in your life, how you feel about it, and if there's anything you'd like to see change as you continue to work through this guide.

Spiritual exhaustion:

Physical exhaustion:

Mental exhaustion:

Emotional exhaustion:

## Low Power Mode Plan

In chapter 1 of *Tired of Being Tired*, I write:

> If you have an iPhone, you're probably familiar with Low Power Mode. When your battery hits 20 percent or lower, a notification will pop up asking if you'd like to switch to Low Power Mode. Once your phone is in this mode, it uses less of the battery in order to conserve your power longer, but it also internally powers down a little—by not using its full capabilities.
>
> You can't really tell from the outside, as a user, that the phone is in Low Power Mode. But internally, it's doing less and saving up.

People, as it turns out, have a Low Power Mode option as well. We have to be intentional about engaging it and sticking with it. And when we do, we can find bits of reprieve from our exhaustion.

For this section, I have two Low Power Mode suggestions, which you'll also find in chapters 1 and 3:

- Notice anytime you feel shame about your fatigue. Conserve some of your precious spiritual, physical, mental, or emotional energy by reminding yourself that feeling tired is not a problem you caused. You did not start this fight.
- Maybe for the time that it takes you to work through this book, ask God to help you put the rest of your skepticism down. To be honest, it takes a lot of energy to critique a process while you're in it. So, what if, for however long you're working through this book, you commit to not spending your precious energy on doubting whether you'll ever stop feeling tired.

Spend some time writing down your plan for practicing these Low Power Mode options. You might consider the following:

- Listing signs (could be spiritual, physical, mental, or emotional) that you need to engage Low Power Mode
- Jotting down names of a few people who can encourage or support you when you're running on a lower battery
- Choosing a place—maybe your phone's lock screen or a sticky note on the fridge—to put reminders that it's okay to conserve your energy sometimes

## Set the Script

Later in the book and study guide, we'll work on developing language for communicating our need for support, saying no, and drawing boundaries with others. For this initial session, let's set the script for how we're going to speak to ourselves—what our internal monologues will sound like—as we reckon with our relationship with tiredness, exhaustion, and energy.

As you take the time to read and reflect, allow yourself to access Low Power Mode, and let yourself prioritize rest, you may find your inner critic getting loud. Maybe she'll say you're not doing enough, that you're just wanting an excuse to be lazy, or that everyone but you seems to be able to get everything done.

What does your inner critic sound like when you try to rest?

Consider what a succinct, one-sentence truth might sound like in response to your critic. It may be something like:

> "Come to me, all you who are weary and burdened, and I will give you rest." (Matt. 11:28)
>
> "Jesus ate, slept, and wept, so I can too."
>
> "I am made in God's image."

Write your comforting truth here:

## Community Questions

How do you feel about tackling the topic of tiredness?

What patterns of rest and work were modeled for you in childhood?

Read the passage aloud from Genesis 1–2 in the Read and Reflect section. What do you see in the text that reveals God's design for work and rest?

## Prayer

Each session, I'll include a prayer that's drawn from Scripture. Pray these words for yourself, and consider praying them for your group participants, friends, or family members as well.

*God of Rest,*

*Your Son tells us that if we—those of us who are weary and burdened—come to Him, He will give us rest for our souls. We confess that, sometimes, that's hard for us to believe. Thank You for being a God who does not give up on us when we try to live solely in our own strength and forget to rely on Your endless love.*

*Help us to notice when we're exhausted and to come to You. Help us have the humility and courage to acknowledge our own tiredness. Help us listen to Your voice when we're tempted to listen to the voice of pride, shame, or fear.*

*We're coming to You, weary and burdened. We're trusting You to give us rest.*

*Amen.*

# session *two*

First: Read *Tired of Being Tired* chapters 4–6.

## A Note from Jess

Dear friend,

Where does it hurt?

I asked that question at the beginning of chapter 4 of *Tired of Being Tired*. It's the question a friend encouraged me to ask my young son when he became withdrawn at a tender point in his childhood. It's the question that helped him express through tears that his back was hurting—that his emotional pain was manifesting physically in his body.

Maybe as you hear that story, your own places of hurt spring to mind. You may already know that your heart is exhausted with the pain of severed relationships or that your mind is spent from too many days with too many to-do lists. You may be in a season of sleeplessness that leaves you physically worn down, or your soul may feel wrung dry.

Whatever the case, I know this: Jesus meets us in our tiredness. All we have to do is come to Him. We do not serve a God who is disappointed in our need for rest; we serve a God who created our need for rest. There is no shame in acknowledging our fatigue. In fact, such an acknowledgment is a beautiful thing—it's a way of agreeing with God that we are limited and that we need Him.

As you work through this session, may the banner over everything be shame off you. He is not frustrated with you about your fatigue. God is pleased with you, sister. He loves you and He longs to give you rest. Let's honor Him with our honesty about the places where we need His renewal.

Jess

## Savor the Scripture

Whether individually or in a group setting, read this passage aloud, then set a one-minute timer for meditating on it silently.

> Truly my soul finds rest in God;
> my salvation comes from him.
> Truly he is my rock and my salvation;
> he is my fortress, I will never be shaken. (Ps. 62:1–2)

Which word or phrase from the passage is sticking with you after the meditation moment? Jot it down as a guiding theme for the rest of the session.

## Read and Reflect

We know that the whole creation has been groaning as in the pains of childbirth right up to the present time. Not only so, but we ourselves, who have the firstfruits of the Spirit, groan inwardly as we wait eagerly for our adoption to sonship, the redemption of our bodies. For in this hope we were saved. But hope that is seen is no hope at all. Who hopes for what they already have? But if we hope for what we do not yet have, we wait for it patiently.

In the same way, the Spirit helps us in our weakness. We do not know what we ought to pray for, but the Spirit himself intercedes for us through wordless groans. And he who searches our hearts knows the mind of the Spirit, because the Spirit intercedes for God's people in accordance with the will of God.

And we know that in all things God works for the good of those who love him, who have been called according to his purpose. (Rom. 8:22–28)

What can you observe about God in this passage?

What can you observe about us, His children, in this passage?

Why and how does the Spirit help us in our weakness?

## Guided Journaling

Read (or reread) this section from chapter 6, considering it as you journal your thoughts in response to the questions below.

> Can I invite you into an honest moment of prayer right now with your Father?
>
> If you're doubtful that spiritual rest will work for you, tell Him now.
>
> If you're struggling with spiritual exhaustion because of the actions or words of someone you trusted, tell God about it.
>
> If you're wondering why He'd allow you to be so burdened and overloaded, let it out.
>
> If you're weary and burdened and can't see where He's at in this, tell Him.
>
> If you're up against the wall and desperate to know what His yoke is, this is the part where you let it out.
>
> Being brutally honest with God and ourselves is the beginning of fighting exhaustion. If it's real rest we want, then we need to get real with God first. This is the first step to moving away from living in a cycle of fatigue that keeps you from the abundance, freedom, and peace that Jesus purchased for you.
>
> Our Father is with you and for you. He created you with care, love, intention, and wild vision. Our Savior and Friend, Jesus, purchased your freedom and abundance on the cross and rose with

your healing and resurrection in hand. The Spirit that raised Him from the grave rests on us and works within us to help us see the kingdom of God come in our time.

We are not alone. We are not on the hook or needing to fend for ourselves. God is with us and for us. And this is life-changing news.

Even if you feel most exhausted physically, emotionally, or mentally, there's a spiritual component to your fatigue. If you could tell God anything about how you feel spiritually right now, especially as it pertains to tiredness, what would it be?

What lies have you believed about what's expected of you spiritually?

What might repentance from defending yourself look like? Another way to think of it—what might it look like for you to rely on God as your Protector?

## Symptom Checker

If you're reading *Tired of Being Tired* along with working through the study guide, you'll find a quiz in this week's reading (chap. 4) designed to help you identify the area of your life in which you're most exhausted.

In this session, we'll assess ourselves in the area of spiritual exhaustion.

Check any symptoms of spiritual exhaustion that you're experiencing:

- ☐ Striving
- ☐ Fear that you'll disappoint God or step out of His will
- ☐ A distorted or unclear view of the gospel
- ☐ Feeling fear or dread about the afterlife
- ☐ An inability to receive compassion or give it
- ☐ A defeatist mindset about your own life or future

Write out concrete examples of how the symptoms you checked show up in your life. For example:

*Striving:* I volunteer in multiple ministries because it helps me feel confident that I'm growing spiritually. But I think, maybe, I'm actually using those activities to keep from trusting God.

*Feeling fear or dread about the afterlife:* I believe in my mind that my salvation is secure and that I will spend eternity with God, but sometimes I lie awake at night wondering if I'm really saved or if I've sinned too much to receive God's grace.

*An inability to receive compassion or give it:* When I make a mistake, I feel angry that I need to apologize and even more upset if the person I hurt is gracious toward me when I say I'm sorry.

## Low Power Mode Plan

At the end of chapter 6, I give four tips for spiritual Low Power Mode. Let's review them:

- Rethink or retool your time with God: If it currently feels like a "have to," switch it up. If it's an intense study time, try reading something a little lighter. If you always feel guilty about not praying longer, try listening to worship music instead. Go on a walk with God. Try journaling, or take a break from journaling.
- Begin a gratitude practice to fight striving about your season.
- Practice saying you're sorry and don't let guilt steal your humility.
- Confess to others to fight shame.

Spend some time considering which of these Low Power Mode tips resonate with you, or come up with one or two for yourself. Then write down your plan for practicing your Low Power Mode options. Try to get as concrete as possible by listing people, times, places, and things that can help you. For example:

On Tuesday morning, create a playlist of worship music to listen to while I go on a walk.

Take a break from in-depth Bible study. Text [friend] and ask if she'd like to read a psalm each morning, then text or voice-memo about it.

At family dinner on Wednesday, ask spouse/kids to help me grow in offering and accepting apologies and invite them to join in for themselves. Come up with a plan together—something silly like a sticker chart—for growing in offering and accepting sincere apologies and our eagerness to forgive.

## Set the Script

It's time to figure out how to talk to ourselves as we're engaging our spiritual exhaustion. Because the exhaustion is already inside of us, the words we need are words of response—statements that are both strong and gentle corrections of our false beliefs, as well as heartening comforts in our discouragement.

What does your spiritual exhaustion sound like? Check any that apply:

- ☐ I have to do everything for the people around me or I'm failing to serve God.
- ☐ If I skip Bible study or forget to have my devotional time, I'm disappointing God.
- ☐ The gospel is sufficient for my salvation, but I need to do everything I can to prove to Jesus that I was worth His sacrifice.
- ☐ What if I'm not actually saved/good enough to go to heaven?
- ☐ I don't deserve compassion or forgiveness.
- ☐ I don't want to read my Bible or pray, and the guilt over that is drowning me.
- ☐ [Create your own.] ______________________________

Consider what a response to your specific spiritual exhaustion might sound like. While Low Power Mode options cover tangible actions that we can take to address our spiritual tiredness, these Set the Script suggestions pertain specifically to our internal monologues. At the most basic level, we're picking something to repeat to ourselves when fatigue threatens to overtake us with shame and condemnation in hand. These may be words we decide to pray, whisper aloud, or share with our family or friends as a declaration of truth. What matters most is that they are accurate, comforting, and easy to remember when we need to recall the truth.

Scripts for responding to our spiritual exhaustion may include:

"Truly my soul finds rest in God; my salvation comes from Him." (Ps. 62:1)

"God created me to need rest."

"I can honor God's design for me by taking a break from serving."

"I am not the savior of the world. Jesus is the Savior of the world."

What might the script be for responding to your specific experience of spiritual fatigue?

## Community Questions

What does spiritual exhaustion feel like for you?

Describe a time when you felt spiritually rested or replenished. What was happening in your life? What did you feel like? What did God use to bring you rest (this could be a person, place, thing, experience, etc.)?

The Bible describes the afterlife for a believer as "entering into God's rest" (Job 3:17; Rev. 14:13). What do you imagine that rest will be like? What might it look like to see a glimpse of that rest in your life right now?

# Prayer

*God of Renewal,*

*Our spirits are tired. We want to honor You. We want to proclaim Your name, live according to Your truth, and bless the world the way You have blessed us. We confess that sometimes these desires become disconnected from the truth of who You are and how You made us. Sometimes we want to take the world by storm more than we want You to calm the storms inside of us. We repent of taking beautiful things You have given us—relationships, ministries, opportunities—and treating them as invitations to strive and prove ourselves rather than gifts to steward and enjoy.*

*Will You bring us rest? Will You help us to recall Your compassion and kindness and to speak words of life to ourselves and others? Will You give us grace, and help us to give grace to ourselves when we inevitably fail in this area again? Help us, even as we stumble, to make our way to the green pastures You have given us, that we might lie down in them.*

*Amen.*

# session *three*

First: Read *Tired of Being Tired* chapters 7–8.

## A Note from Jess

Dear friend,

In a world that craves knowledge and praises productivity, the thought of rest can feel truly terrifying. *What will happen if I take a break? Who will judge me if I don't answer the phone? When will everything get done if I shut down for a week?*

I get it. I have asked all of these questions at various times throughout my life. I've made the wrong choices because I feared the repercussions if I chose to say no when others (or I) thought I should say yes.

I've also experienced the freedom of choosing rest, quiet, and recovery. There is a confident, powerful peace that comes with realizing that the questions we ask ourselves can change. Instead of asking, *What will fall apart if I press pause?* I am learning to ask, *What does it look like to agree with God that my body needs rest?*

Changes the paradigm, doesn't it? Of course, as simple as that shift may sound, there's nothing easy about putting it into practice. But that's where Holy Spirit, the will to try again after failure, and the power of community can make such a significant difference in our lives. They certainly have in mine. And I'm praying that, as you work through this section on physical rest, you'll find yourself feeling empowered and equipped to pursue physical rest with the certainty that God smiles upon your pursuit.

Jess

## Savor the Scripture

Whether individually or in a group setting, read this passage aloud, then set a one-minute timer for meditating on it silently.

> Unless the LORD builds the house,
> the builders labor in vain.
> Unless the LORD watches over the city,
> the guards stand watch in vain.
> In vain you rise early
> and stay up late,
> toiling for food to eat—
> for he grants sleep to those he loves. (Ps. 127:1–2)

Which word or phrase from the passage is sticking with you after the meditation moment? Jot it down as a guiding theme for the rest of the session.

## Read and Reflect

When Jesus came into Peter's house, he saw Peter's mother-in-law lying in bed with a fever. He touched her hand and the fever left her, and she got up and began to wait on him.

When evening came, many who were demon-possessed were brought to him, and he drove out the spirits with a word and healed all the sick. This was to fulfill what was spoken through the prophet Isaiah:

> "He took up our infirmities
> and bore our diseases."

When Jesus saw the crowd around him, he gave orders to cross to the other side of the lake. Then a teacher of the law came to him and said, "Teacher, I will follow you wherever you go."

Jesus replied, "Foxes have dens and birds have nests, but the Son of Man has no place to lay his head."

Another disciple said to him, "Lord, first let me go and bury my father."

But Jesus told him, "Follow me, and let the dead bury their own dead."

Then he got into the boat and his disciples followed him. Suddenly a furious storm came up on the lake, so that the waves swept over the boat. But Jesus was sleeping. The disciples went and woke him, saying, "Lord, save us! We're going to drown!"

He replied, "You of little faith, why are you so afraid?" Then he got up and rebuked the winds and the waves, and it was completely calm.

The men were amazed and asked, "What kind of man is this? Even the winds and the waves obey him!" (Matt. 8:14–27)

What was Jesus doing before He got in the boat?

How would you describe the disciples' reaction when they saw Jesus sleeping?

How does Jesus's response to the disciples speak to your thoughts on physical rest?

## Guided Journaling

Read (or reread) this section from chapter 8, considering it as you journal your thoughts in response to the questions below.

> Only you can figure out and determine your personal borders and boundaries, and then only you can create rhythms in your life that honor them. So, think of this less as a task looming over you and more as an opportunity to reconnect with who God made you to be, to listen to and learn from the beautiful limitations of your body so you can honor them worshipfully.
>
> Here are some questions to get you started:
>
> - How much sleep is optimal for you in this season?
> - Can you begin setting a standard bedtime routine and hour to honor the biblical principle of evening and then morning, rest then work?
> - What food and exercise practices leave you feeling renewed?
> - Where do you most need quiet and time to regroup in your day? How can you work that in?
> - Where can you build in rhythmic rest weekly, quarterly, and yearly?

Which of the questions above feels most challenging for you to answer?

If you were to set your intentions on building a habit in response to one of the questions above, which habit feels like the right one to start with? What would it look like for you to build and stick with that new routine?

How did your family of origin approach physical rest?

## Symptom Checker

In this session, we'll check in with ourselves in the area of physical exhaustion.

Check any symptoms of physical exhaustion that you're experiencing:

- ☐ Yawning, headaches, dizziness, sore muscles
- ☐ Saying yes because no one else will
- ☐ Always arriving early or staying late out of obligation

- ☐ Sleep sabotage: staying up later than is wise to get time for yourself
- ☐ Moodiness or irritability
- ☐ Feeling like you can't be fully present

Write out concrete examples of how the symptoms you checked show up in your life. For example:

*Saying yes because no one else will:* I didn't want to sign up for two PTA committees, but no one else was stepping up. I felt like I had to. It's for the kids!

*Always arriving early or staying late out of obligation:* I'm always the one showing up before the crowd and staying after they leave, whether it's for a ministry event, party, or volunteer project. There's always something to do, and someone has to do it.

*Feeling like you can't be fully present:* When I'm working, I get distracted by thoughts of my personal life. When I'm trying to relax at home, I'm thinking about my volunteer responsibilities. Even in conversations I care about, I find myself wanting to retreat or accomplish another task.

## Low Power Mode Plan

When it comes to physical exhaustion, I have several Low Power Mode suggestions, which you'll also find in chapter 8 of *Tired of Being Tired*:

- Pause before saying yes to anything, no matter how simple it seems. Truly pray about the decision if you need to, and ask, *If I say yes to this, what is my reason for doing so?*
- Prioritize going to sleep well, not just waking up well (rest before work for your body).
- Normalize participation over performance. When you show up somewhere, pay attention to ways you may be trying to perform (your appearance, being early, being eager, trying to affect others' perception of you).
- Save your mental energy and rewrite the narrative when you talk about your physical limitations (your need for sleep, time off, quiet, etc.). Try not to apologize, explain, or talk negatively about your basic physical needs.

Spend some time considering which of these Low Power Mode tips resonate with you, or come up with one or two for yourself. Then write down your plan for practicing your Low Power Mode options. Try to get as concrete as possible by listing people, times, places, and things that can help you. For example:

Rather than falling asleep on the couch when I can no longer keep my eyes open, I'll intentionally get into bed at 9:30, when I'm still alert, so that I can read for half an hour before going to sleep.

I will make a list of things that are an automatic yes, an automatic no, and an automatic "let me think about that," then stick with it.

Before I go to work, church, school, or anywhere I'm likely to be asked to take on additional tasks, I will practice communicating my limits with kindness but without apology.

## Set the Script

While our spiritual script-setting revolved around how we speak to ourselves, during this session we're going to focus on how to talk to others when we're physically exhausted. Setting boundaries can feel challenging and even taboo in some social or ministry circles, which can lead to a lot of angst and shame within ourselves when we need to say no. But the fact remains—there are times when we need to say no or "not now." So, let's figure out how to do that.

Write out a few scenarios when boundary-setting may be necessary for you. Examples may include:

At the office, my boss knows that I'm reliable and hardworking, which leads to her asking me to take on a lot of additional tasks.

I feel pressured to show up at every church event, even though this season of my life makes it difficult to do so.

My friend group is filled with extroverts who have more capacity than I do for spending time together. I worry that if

I say no to an evening together, they'll think I don't want to hang out with them.

Now, let's figure out a statement or two that you can keep in your back pocket for when it's time to say no. You may feel uncomfortable, anxious, or even afraid to set a boundary. Choosing words to use beforehand won't take every negative emotion away, but it can help you speak up anyway. Check a statement or two that feels sayable for you:

- ☐ "Thank you so much for asking, but I'm unable to do that."
- ☐ "I don't have the bandwidth for that, but I'm honored you asked."
- ☐ "I'm not available to make it. Thank you for asking!"

- ☐ "Thank you for thinking of me. I wish I were able to, but I'm not."
- ☐ "I can't make it; thanks, though!"
- ☐ "I wish I could, but I can't do that at this time."
- ☐ "Please ask me again some other time. In this season that won't work for me."
- ☐ "I love spending time with you, but I need a quiet night/ weekend. Let's try again soon!"
- ☐ [Create your own.] ______________________________

## Community Questions

What does physical exhaustion feel like in your body?

How do you perceive that your Father responds to your physical exhaustion?

How might honoring your physical tiredness help you learn more about God and yourself?

# Prayer

*God of Replenishing,*

*On the seventh day, You rested. We read those words and forget them in the same breath, busying ourselves with the next activity. Help us to remember that You, a perfect God with endless supply, chose to rest. Help us to pattern our lives after the model You set in creation and in the embodiment of Your truth in the life of Jesus, who healed hearts and bodies and then slept through a storm.*

*Teach us to say no to another task when our bodies call for our attention. Teach us to rely on You for strength when we know we are in desperate need of a nap or a night alone but we do not know when they will be possible. Teach us to disciple one another in the truth of Your Word, which makes plain Your intention for us to work and rest, play and pause, eat and drink, be poured out and sleep in peace.*

*Amen.*

# session *four*

First: Read *Tired of Being Tired* chapters 9–10.

## A Note from Jess

Dear friend,

Peace is our birthright.

As I began to actively fight mental exhaustion in my own life, that's the truth I kept returning to time and time again. The pace and demands of our daily lives often seem to tell us that anxiety and overwhelm are foregone conclusions we just have to endure. But the Bible makes it plain that while our mental state in this life may not be easy to manage, it can still be defined by peace because we worship a God of peace.

As you work through this session, my prayer for you is that the peace that surpasses all understanding will be your guiding light. If there is anything you take from the coming pages, I hope it's the certainty that your identity is secure as a child of God—that can have a profound impact on our lives. When you struggle to come to a decision in a few hours, or tomorrow brings a series of challenges you simply don't know how to think about, I pray that you will come back to your identity and your birthright.

You belong to God. And because you're His daughter, peace is your birthright. No calendar, schedule, or to-do list is allowed to stand against what God says is true about who you are. May that truth comfort and lead you away from mental exhaustion and into the abundance God has for you.

Jess

## Savor the Scripture

Whether individually or in a group setting, read this passage aloud, then set a one-minute timer for meditating on it silently.

> You will keep in perfect peace
> those whose minds are steadfast,
> because they trust in you. (Isa. 26:3)

Which word or phrase from the passage is sticking with you after the meditation moment? Jot it down as a guiding theme for the rest of the session.

## Read and Reflect

> Rejoice in the Lord always. I will say it again: Rejoice! Let your gentleness be evident to all. The Lord is near. Do not be anxious about anything, but in every situation, by prayer and petition, with thanksgiving, present your requests to God. And the peace of God, which transcends all understanding, will guard your hearts and your minds in Christ Jesus.

> Finally, brothers and sisters, whatever is true, whatever is noble, whatever is right, whatever is pure, whatever is lovely, whatever is admirable—if anything is excellent or praiseworthy—think about such things. Whatever you have learned or received or heard from me, or seen in me—put it into practice. And the God of peace will be with you.
>
> I rejoiced greatly in the Lord that at last you renewed your concern for me. Indeed, you were concerned, but you had no opportunity to show it. I am not saying this because I am in need, for I have learned to be content whatever the circumstances. I know what it is to be in need, and I know what it is to have plenty. I have learned the secret of being content in any and every situation, whether well fed or hungry, whether living in plenty or in want. I can do all this through him who gives me strength. (Phil. 4:4–13)

What does Paul exhort the Philippians to do when they are anxious?

It's our time to shine, list makers. What types of things does Paul encourage the Philippians to think about?

Based on the preceding verses, what do you think Paul means by "the secret of being content" toward the end of the passage?

## Guided Journaling

Read (or reread) this section from chapter 10, considering it as you journal your thoughts in response to the questions below.

> Whether it's a quick check-in with my heart early in the morning, a family vacation, a stressful meeting at work, or a worshipful encounter at a women's conference, I want to live in the present and practice being fully awake right where I'm at. I'm assuming you do too. So, this is how we'll spend less energy processing what took place and conserve strength and vitality for what's to come.
>
> 1. *Notice what's happening.* Engage all five senses, capture, pay attention, and enjoy. How does that stack of papers feel in your hand during the meeting? What does that dinner you're cooking smell like? What colors do you notice on the walk with your friend? How does the ground feel beneath your feet as you stand to worship in church? What does your toddler's laugh sound like as you tickle them before bed?
>
>    You can stay in the moment when you notice the moment. But to engage your mind meaningfully, take this further than literally. Notice how you feel, where your mind is wandering when it wanders, how the space you're in feels

spiritually, and what seems to be happening underneath the surface.

2. *Say thanks, and express gratitude.* To keep our minds practicing our own presence and the presence of God, we can live out Psalm 16:6 and declare that the boundary lines have fallen in pleasant places for us. Think of things you're grateful for and keep a list of them on your phone, list them in your head in prayer, or say them out loud to a friend.
3. *Accept how it is.* One reason our brains fight so hard to ruminate in the past or skip ahead to the future and then end up exhausted is that we don't often love what we're experiencing in the present. Instead, we wish it was how it used to be, or we hope it will shift into something else in the future.

   But one way we can take some mental energy back is to accept how things are in the moment, knowing that God's power is made perfect in weakness and the miraculous is often found in the mundane.

Describe a time when you realized you were *not* staying in the moment. Where was your mind?

Describe a time when you encountered distraction and stayed in the moment. What helped you focus? What did your mind feel like during that event?

Think about the week to come and choose a time or two when you want to practice staying in the moment. What might it look like for you to notice what's around you in those settings?

## Symptom Checker

In this session, we'll check in with ourselves in the area of mental exhaustion.

Check any symptoms of mental exhaustion that you're experiencing:

- ☐ Stress headaches
- ☐ Trouble sleeping
- ☐ Feeling confused or behind

- ☐ Numbing out
- ☐ Poor memory or cognitive function
- ☐ Feeling panicked or anxious

Write out concrete examples of how the symptoms you checked show up in your life. For example:

*Stress headaches:* By Wednesday afternoon nearly every week, I feel a headache starting to brew. It's like my mind is already exhausted from everything it's had to process that week, and it's only halfway over.

*Trouble sleeping:* No matter how physically tired I am, at least a few nights a week I find myself unable to fall asleep because I simply cannot stop thinking. Sometimes the thoughts are big worries or fears, but sometimes it's just my to-do list running on a loop in my head. I can't turn it off.

*Numbing out:* Whenever I have a moment that's not claimed by a task or activity, all I want to do is watch TV or Tik-Tok. The thought of engaging my mind in something that's actually enriching feels like too much effort. I'd rather just stop thinking altogether.

## Low Power Mode Plan

When it comes to mental exhaustion, I have seven Low Power Mode suggestions, which you'll also find in chapter 10:

- Utilize brain dumps (one minute of writing down everything on your mind) to clarify what is clogging your energy.
- Set timers to focus on or finish tasks, and play around with rewards to create brain satisfaction when you're done.
- Assign days or times to tasks, concerns, or responsibilities so that you don't live like you must do everything all at once.
- Take social media and/or news media breaks when needed.

- Turn on read receipts for emails and text messages; open them only when you have time and margin to respond.
- Normalize taking longer to make decisions.
- Block sites or apps that you find distracting so you can break the innate urge to open or visit those pages.

Spend some time considering which of these Low Power Mode tips resonate with you, or come up with one or two for yourself. Then write down your plan for practicing your Low Power Mode options. Try to get as concrete as possible by listing people, times, places, and things that can help you. For example:

On Saturday afternoon, when I typically start feeling anxious about the weekend going so fast, do a brain dump, then choose one task to complete.

Take a social media break this weekend.

Create a chore checklist for Monday through Friday with two tasks for each day. Choose rewards for each completion.

_______________________________________________

_______________________________________________

_______________________________________________

_______________________________________________

_______________________________________________

_______________________________________________

_______________________________________________

## Set the Script

It's time to figure out how to talk to ourselves as we're engaging our mental exhaustion. First, let's determine what our internal monologue tells us when we're tired.

When you are mentally fatigued, which of the following statements sound like your inner voice? Check any that apply:

- ☐ I am a nervous wreck, what is wrong with me?
- ☐ I'm so dumb. No one else would have made that mistake.
- ☐ My memory is horrible.
- ☐ I don't know how to say what I'm thinking. I'm not sure I even know what I'm thinking.
- ☐ There's no time for me to pursue what I love. I can't even meet my obligations!
- ☐ I need to turn on music or a show when things get quiet. I don't like the thoughts I have to face in the silence otherwise.
- ☐ [Create your own.] ______________________________

Consider what a response to your specific mental exhaustion might sound like. Keep in mind that this specific area of exhaustion can make it hard to recall words or phrases, so short scripts are probably the way to go. The point isn't to address every last false belief or discouragement in one statement. Instead, the scripts we set for responding to our mental exhaustion simply need to guide us to the truth—that it's okay to be tired and that our brains were created for rest.

Scripts for responding to our mental exhaustion may include:

"Father, I release everyone and everything to You."*

"I am grateful for ____."

"Peace is my birthright."

"I am allowed to take a break."

What might the script be for responding to your specific experience of mental fatigue?

*This is a prayer that my husband, Nick, and I learned from John Eldredge, *Get Your Life Back: Everyday Practices for a World Gone Mad* (Nashville: Thomas Nelson, 2020), 16.

## Community Questions

What, if any, have been your experiences with practicing silence and/or solitude?

What makes you passionate, and what might it look like to give that passion more focus?

What do you need to release in order to create space for mental rest?

## Prayer

*God of Restoration,*

*We confess that sometimes we try to live as though our brains are robots with no need for reprieve. We try to remember everything, solve everything, understand everything.*

*Help us to embrace our finite minds, which we can do only by trusting in Your infinite nature.*

*Help us to remember that peace is our birthright.*

*Help us to give ourselves grace when we forget something that matters.*

*Help us to orient our minds around the truth of Your Word.*

*Help us to embrace silence, solitude, and presence rather than fear them.*

*We long to be kept in Your perfect peace with our minds stayed on You. May we return to You for our every need, again and again.*

*Amen.*

# session *five*

First: Read *Tired of Being Tired* chapters 11–12.

## A Note from Jess

Dear friend,

I'm willing to bet that if you're not in a season of emotional overwhelm, you have been in the past. Life piles up and our ways of coping don't always work as well as we'd like. Some of us experience our feelings in big, acute ways in real time. Others find themselves suddenly crying or scared weeks, months, or even years after an emotionally difficult situation has occurred.

The purpose of this session is not to figure out how to manage our emotions, if by "manage" we mean learn how to shove them in a drawer. It's also not our goal to arrive at the conclusion that our feelings are always right and should be our guide. Instead, my prayer is that this session will give you comfort, wisdom, and hope for living as an emotional being in light of an emotional God.

Does that sound weird to you—the idea of an emotional God? If so, I get it. We tend to think of "emotional" as "overly emotional." But God is an emotional being. How could He not be if we, emotional creatures, are made in His image? Trusting that

God designed feelings for a reason, let's enter into this session with a clear objective: honoring our emotions and welcoming God into them.

Amen?

Jess

## Savor the Scripture

Whether individually or in a group setting, read this passage aloud, then set a one-minute timer for meditating on it silently.

> The Lord is my strength and my shield;
> my heart trusts in him, and he helps me.
> My heart leaps for joy,
> and with my song I praise him. (Ps. 28:7)

Which word or phrase from the passage is sticking with you after the meditation moment? Jot it down as a guiding theme for the rest of the session.

## Read and Reflect

> I cry aloud to the Lord;
> I lift up my voice to the Lord for mercy.
> I pour out before him my complaint;
> before him I tell my trouble.
>
> When my spirit grows faint within me,
> it is you who watch over my way.

In the path where I walk
  people have hidden a snare for me.
Look and see, there is no one at my right hand;
  no one is concerned for me.
I have no refuge;
  no one cares for my life.

I cry to you, LORD;
  I say, "You are my refuge,
  my portion in the land of the living."

Listen to my cry,
  for I am in desperate need;
rescue me from those who pursue me,
  for they are too strong for me.
Set me free from my prison,
  that I may praise your name.
Then the righteous will gather about me
  because of your goodness to me. (Ps. 142)

What do you observe about God in this passage?

What do you learn about the psalmist and his situation in the passage?

How might this passage shape the way you express your emotional exhaustion to God?

## Guided Journaling

Read (or reread) this section from chapter 12, considering it as you journal your thoughts in response to the questions below.

> I propose we choose compassionate curiosity as an approach to our feelings. Compassionate curiosity is not beating ourselves up, shaming ourselves, or trying to stuff our feelings down but rather paying attention to them with interested hearts to figure out why they've arrived. Compassionate curiosity isn't obeying every feeling. It's not blindly following every feeling to destruction—but instead noticing it, naming it, and discerning the best way to move forward.

Let's walk through this:

Notice what you feel as the emotion hits. How does the anger, excitement, fear, disappointment, or other feeling appear in your body? Notice it with God, involve Him in the process, and ask Holy Spirit to help you discern where this emotion might be coming from and what's making it so strong, or track when you often find yourself experiencing this feeling.

Name the emotion as best you can. Don't fear using nonfeeling words, metaphors, or other adjectives to get as specific as possible. If it's as straightforward as "jealousy," you can just use that word. But if it's as subtle as "a sticky sadness twinged with fear," that's great too. I remember describing my grief as "pinching rather than punching," and the friend I was speaking to immediately understood what I was trying to convey. Give yourself the same space to name what it is you're experiencing.

Finally, take time to discern the wisest way to move forward concerning this emotion. Does it need confession because it came from an unhealthy or unholy root belief? Do you need to sit with God and allow Him to comfort you? Is there something you can or should do to take a step to resolve a conflict or issue that's causing the emotion? Do you need to let it go or talk it out with someone else? What is God saying to you about this feeling?

Reflect on an emotion you've been experiencing recently. What does it feel like in your body? How would you describe the feeling to someone who has never experienced it?

Imagine that you are holding your emotion in your hands. What does it look like? Does it have a texture or scent? What color is it?

Picture yourself handing the object of your emotion to Jesus. What does it look like in His hands? What does He say to you as He holds it? How do you feel watching Him hold it?

## Symptom Checker

In this session, we'll check in with ourselves in the area of emotional exhaustion.

Check any symptoms of emotional exhaustion that you're experiencing:

- ☐ Irritability
- ☐ Apathy
- ☐ Unprovoked tears or anger

- ☐ Physical fatigue or soreness
- ☐ Depression
- ☐ Sense of dread or hopelessness

Write out concrete examples of how the symptoms you checked show up in your life. For example:

*Apathy:* On Thursday night, not a single part of me wanted to go to book club. It's typically the evening I look forward to most each week, but I could not conjure up any positive feelings about it. I just felt . . . blah.

*Unprovoked tears or anger:* Ten minutes into my commute yesterday, I felt my eyes welling up with tears and I didn't know why. I cried the entire rest of the way to work.

*Physical fatigue or soreness:* Even though I've been taking good care of my body, it hurts in ways that are hard to address. My neck and shoulders ache no matter how often I stretch.

## Low Power Mode Plan

When it comes to emotional exhaustion, I have nine Low Power Mode suggestions, which you'll also find in chapter 12:

- Create a journaling habit. This is a great way to notice, process, and make space for your emotions.
- Pay attention to patterns in emotions. See if you can use less energy being surprised by them and instead anticipate their arrival in health.
- Ask God if He has anything He wants to share with you about __________ emotion. Listen for His voice, search His Word, and look for Him to give you insight.
- Dance it out. Just like Cristina and Meredith on *Grey's Anatomy* (if you know, you know). Put on some life-giving music and see if those emotions don't start to come to the surface.
- If you're feeling grief but have stuffed down your emotions so long you can't access them, try watching a sad movie to connect your physical and mental.

- Likewise, I suggest watching something hilarious if you have difficulty tapping into your emotions. Laughing, like crying, also stimulates endorphins.
- Play this game with some trusted friends: Send three emojis via text to tell each other how you're doing. No need for explanation, just an unapologetic emotional check-in.
- Utilize a period tracker app or keep a quick note on your phone to anticipate and accommodate hormonal shifts.
- Consider shifting the main lifestyle factors that impact emotional health: exercise, nutrition, and alcohol consumption. While making initial changes may take effort, the energy that will be saved in the long haul will surely make this a low-power move.

Spend some time considering which of these Low Power Mode tips resonate with you, or come up with one or two for yourself. Then write down your plan for practicing your Low Power Mode options. Try to get as concrete as possible by listing people, times, places, and things that can help you. For example:

Start a group text with Sarah, Laura, and Kate where we share our three emojis.

Download a period tracker and turn on push notifications so I take time to check in hormonally each day.

Spend ten minutes before bed each night journaling.

## Set the Script

Whether we tend to stuff our emotions, excuse them away, or shout them from the rooftops, chances are that we all have some less than healthy inner language about our feelings. Let's take some time to describe the ways we talk to ourselves about our emotions.

What does your internal monologue sound like when it comes to how you think about your feelings? Check any that apply:

- ☐ I'm fine!
- ☐ Crying is so dumb. What's the point?
- ☐ I don't want to talk to anyone about how I'm feeling because I don't want to be a downer.
- ☐ I have no reason to feel this way. Think about how much worse things could be!
- ☐ No one understands me.
- ☐ I feel angry/sad/frustrated/misunderstood, so I have every right to act that way.
- ☐ I can't feel anything at all.
- ☐ [Create your own.] ____________________

Consider what a response to your emotional exhaustion might sound like. How can you honor your emotions and speak inviting words to yourself? As you set your script, remember that God is the designer of emotions. That does not mean that every feeling we have is from God. But it does mean that dismissing our emotions out of hand is an act that does not align with how God made us. Neither does obeying our emotions without a second thought. Let's set our scripts in a way that acknowledges emotions for what they are, which could sound something like:

"Feeling so much does not make me weak."

"It's okay to feel _____."

"This emotion is real, but it does not define who I am."

"The Lord is close to the brokenhearted and saves those who are crushed in spirit." (Ps. 34:18)

What might the script be for responding to your specific experience of emotional fatigue?

## Community Questions

How did your family of origin talk about or display emotions?

How do unprocessed emotions show up in your life?

How does the thought of inviting God into your emotions strike you?

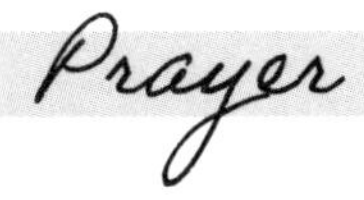

*God of Rejuvenation,*

*We confess that our hearts are tired. Our emotions overwhelm us sometimes, tempting us to obey them or ignore them. Help us to be people who remember that You created emotions and that You intend for them to be one part of our vibrant, abundant lives.*

*Teach us to honor our emotions and to bring them to You. Give us courage to ask for help when we need it. Help us to identify the unprocessed emotions that need our attention and empower us to address them in light of Your love and truth.*

*Amen.*

# session *six*

First: Read *Tired of Being Tired* chapters 13–15.

## A Note from Jess

Dear friend,

I started chapter 1 of *Tired of Being Tired* with this statement: "Every woman I know is tired."

I'm under no illusions that working through this study has changed that fact. I don't think I wrote the magic words that will suddenly *abracadabra* each of us out of fatigue and into endless energy. But here's what I do picture:

Women who are convinced that peace is their birthright.

Women who worship a God of rest.

Women who know they'll continue to make mistakes as they journey away from exhaustion.

Women who trust that the well of living water never runs dry.

Women who support one another in pursuing lives of abundance.

In this final session, we'll reflect on what we've learned together. May we find great joy, comfort, and strength in our spirits, bodies, minds, and hearts.

Jess

## Savor the Scripture

Whether individually or in a group setting, read this passage aloud, then set a one-minute timer for meditating on it silently.

> Finally, brothers and sisters, rejoice! Strive for full restoration, encourage one another, be of one mind, live in peace. And the God of love and peace will be with you. (2 Cor. 13:11)

Which word or phrase from the passage is sticking with you after the meditation moment? Jot it down as a guiding theme for the rest of the session.

---

---

## Read and Reflect

> I saw the Holy City, the new Jerusalem, coming down out of heaven from God, prepared as a bride beautifully dressed for her husband. And I heard a loud voice from the throne saying, "Look! God's dwelling place is now among the people, and he will dwell with them. They will be his people, and God himself will be with them and be their God. 'He will wipe every tear from their eyes. There will be no more death' or mourning or crying or pain, for the old order of things has passed away."
>
> He who was seated on the throne said, "I am making everything new!" Then he said, "Write this down, for these words are trustworthy and true."
>
> He said to me: "It is done. I am the Alpha and the Omega, the Beginning and the End. To the thirsty I will give water without cost from the spring of the water of life. Those who are victorious

> will inherit all this, and I will be their God and they will be my children. (Rev. 21:2–7)

How does this description of the world to come influence your perspective on rest now?

What do you long to see God make new?

What might it look like to live as "those who are victorious" today?

## Guided Journaling

Read (or reread) these questions from chapter 15, journaling in response.

Am I currently tired, and if so, in what way?

How do I perceive God's posture toward me and my exhaustion?

Are there any feelings weighing down my spirit that require confession, wisdom, or action on my part? If so, what are they?

Do I believe God gives rest to those He loves?

## Symptom Checker

At the beginning of this study guide, we jotted down our initial reactions to each category of exhaustion. Let's do a post-study check-in here, documenting how we feel in each area.

There are no wrong answers. All that matters is honesty. Simply jot down your reaction to each category now, stream-of-consciousness style. Try to lift your pen from the page only when you're moving from one type of exhaustion to the next. In other words, share your unfiltered thoughts about how each type of exhaustion shows up in your life, and if you've seen any shifts as you've worked through this guide.

Spiritual exhaustion:

Physical exhaustion:

Mental exhaustion:

Emotional exhaustion:

## Low Power Mode Plan

Refresh your memory about the Low Power Mode suggestions for spiritual (p. 32), physical (p. 46), mental (pp. 60–61), and emotional (pp. 74–75) exhaustion. Choose one suggestion (or your own idea) to carry with you for each area of fatigue. Then write out a plan that you can take with you in the coming weeks or months.

For example:

> This fall, I will start keeping a gratitude journal that I will update at the end of each day. I'll also go to bed by 10:00 on weeknights and take a social media break for a twenty-four-hour period every month. Finally, I will include talking

to God about my emotional state in my prayer time, asking Him for insight into my feelings.

## Set the Script

In chapter 15 of *Tired of Being Tired*, I include several suggestions for language shifts that may communicate peace and shift the culture around you. Consider which of these changes you'd like to make and what it may sound like to do so:

Instead of saying, "I'll sleep when I'm dead," I'll practice saying, "I'm working on prioritizing rest."

Instead of saying, "I'm a people pleaser. It's just who I am," I'll practice saying, "I love to help others, but God is teaching me to receive as well."

Your turn! Fill in the blanks:

Instead of saying, "______________________________," I'll practice saying "______________________________."

## Community Questions

How has this study helped you address your deepest areas of exhaustion?

What is one restful habit you intend to build?

How can you participate in encouraging others and being encouraged to receive rest?

## Prayer

*God of Replenishment,*

*We are grateful. We thank You for the ways that You have shown us how we seek to rely on ourselves. We thank You for reminding us that You are ever present, longing to give us the comfort and rest we crave.*

*Help us to live in light of Your truth and love. When we forget to rely on You, may Your grace bring us back, over and over again. Give us the eyes to see those around us who are desperate for Your peace, and help us to live as those who are confident that peace is our birthright so that others might see Your Spirit in us.*

*We love You. We trust You to provide rest for our souls.*

*Amen.*

Jess Connolly

is the author of several books, including *You Are the Girl for the Job* and *Breaking Free from Body Shame*, and co-author of *Wild and Free*. She and her husband, Nick, planted Bright City Church in Charleston, South Carolina, where they live with their four children. As the lead coach and founder of Go + Tell Gals and the host of *The Jess Connolly Podcast*, Jess wants to leave her generation more in awe of God than she found it. She's passionate about her family, discipling women, God's Word, and the local church.

Connect with Jess

JessConnolly.com

 Jess Connolly

 JessAConnolly

 JessAConnolly